the forced hush of quiet

kendall a. bell

Maverick Duck Press

© 2019

www.maverickduckpress.com

First Edition

Cover art by Kendall A. Bell

ISBN-13: 978-0-578-56631-3

- *For Christinia*

I.   The unquenched thirst, the exposed, beating muscle in the chest

II.   The shadowboxers burned into wallpaper as silhouettes, as ghosts

III. Shattered mirrors and blackened Polaroids

IV. The shards that remain, scattered over dirt and asphalt

V.   When a body becomes invisible, becomes air

I.   ***The unquenched thirst, the exposed, beating muscle
in the chest***

In her kiss, I taste the revolution

the extended middle finger to anyone
and everyone who could deny that our
cause is right and divine. We will
march liplocked into battle. We will
watch the buildings crumble around us,
hear the whistle of gunfire above us.
We will create explosions that devastate
cities without passion, without the pure
want of desire. In her kiss, the birth
of daybreak, the cusp of nirvana.

Sometimes, love is surgery

It is extracting the bitterness that
builds up in the stomach, a festering
cancer cured only with compromise.
It is mending a bone with metal screws
under the anesthesia of compassion.
It is how the removal of a bad organ
can lead to a replacement, the renewal
of tenderness, of rebirth.

Two of Us on the Run

You stare out the window watching buildings
and trees in fast forward and occasionally
nudge my arm, slide your hand down to lace
with mine. You tell me that you have to pee,
and we run in and out of fast food places
just to flush and run without buying anything.
I watch you sleep under yellowing white sheets
that have been washed over and over, while the
clothes we were in are draped over a chair with
bruised wood. We do it all over again in the
morning over countless refills of coffee in a
Waffle House across the highway, your feet stuck
into weathered sneakers and I can smell the vanilla
lotion on your legs as I rest my head in your lap
as you drive, feel your softness against my bristled
face. You drive fast, thinking about the things we
left behind—overdue rent, bosses calling us a no-call/
no-show, names that no one remembers to call. Our
eyes are the open highway, are the stories yet
unwritten.

Where I begin and you end

I know the channels in your head are on
all the time, at the same time. Remember
that I am the tuner, the one who will sort
through that static, the infomercials and
Spanish language stations, and be a constant.
I will not need to be reminded every hour
that you love me - we will be weightless.
Wordless moments on the sofa with the vents
pushing out cool air on a summer evening,
our warm flesh entangled while we gaze into
a sky that stretches into endless evenings
will suffice. Your words will blend with my
words and this collaboration will birth
something profound and lasting. There will
be intensity. Our static bodies at night will
race on the inside, be the beginning and end
of each moment, each breath.

The sweetest honeybee in the hive

You are the orange light breaking through the blue
and black of morning. You are the first drip of
maple syrup over pancakes. You are the crackling
of a fire pit on a summer night. You are the smell
of blueberry coffee in the afternoon. You are the
blinking light on my cellphone, the message I've
waited all day for. You are the sound of evening
in a screened in porch with fireflies watching our
skin touching. You are the thunderstorm rattling
my insides, the smell of rain, the fingers around
mine. You are breakfast in bed, over and over.

A precheck for truth

A single fingertip moving from the base
of your wrist, to the middle of your hand,
where the heat rests, to your fingertips,
that once rested on my hand, that once tapped
out the words that pulled me in like fishing
nets cast in deep, salty water. I search each
centimeter of cells, use a magnifying glass to
mine the proclamations of love they once dragged
in ink, over paper, in smudged slides over a screen.
I disappear in the friction ridges, lost in hope.

That girl is like a sunburn

The sting to the touch above the
collar, the beginning of blisters
on the hairline. The outline of
where her fingers rested while
they were tightly pressed against
your hand. The heat on your face,
on your limbs in the backyard,
when no one is looking. The flush—
breathless racing for shade. The
feel of cool air in the afterglow.

Riptide

Your current hit me in waves,
stung my eyes and left me
murky for days. You were the
taste of salt on my tongue,
the need for quenching. You
left me battered and twisted
on your gritty shores, singed
flesh on a white washed canvas.
This infertile terrain longs
for you to wash over it again.

I can't hold enough of you in my hands

and you keep slipping through my fingers
like sand, like shower water that races
towards a hungry drain. I keep looking
for a wayward string, a belt loop—
anything to grab to keep you near me.
I want you wrapped around me like thick
sheets in winter, like the warmth of
daybreak through the living room window.
This love is like drowning, and you are
the air.

Shutterbug

You are the lightning rod,
the flash in the sky in
mid-afternoon, the long hug
that rumbles through me like
longing, like the distance we
keep. You are all smooth limbs,
all supernova eye brightness,
a widened smile that does not
lie. You capture landscapes
behind a lens, and I picture
being your subject, crouched
on a fallen tree limb, head
just above a nod. I want to
be caught in your sight line,
want to be the caught breath
in the cascade of your warmth.

For A

A ring around the moon is
supposed to be a sign of
rain on the horizon.
Your wishes fall upon the
glowing mass like psalms,
like promise. The radiant
orb will shower them down
to me in the morning.
Whisper again,
whisper again.

Beestung

is an overused metaphor
in reference to lips like
yours, lips that are full,
that could envelop mine.
Who would want a bee or
bees to sting their lips,
to have an affliction to
force glamour? I would tell
you that lips like yours
are the kind I want to kiss
me awake at eight am, to
speak the words "good morning"
and "breakfast in bed". I
would want them to speak in
whispers beneath shared
sheets, under the soft bulbs
of evening. I would want them
singing your favorite songs,
reading your favorite poems,
speaking my favorite sound.

Vines

These branches dip downward-
twist into thickened vines that
cannot be split, cannot unwind.
We are the sweetest entanglement,
the upside-down, superhero movie kiss,
the mourning doves walking together
slowly through morning's wet grass.
We remain a distance away, yet
blissfully tangled.

Until We Get There

We will settle for falling asleep in worn
chairs that have held the frames of people
passing through in fractions. We will count
the change we pluck from underneath the car
seats when we shove them all the way back
searching for a lost a lip balm, pool our
money and use it to buy iced coffee that's
too sweet, but we need the caffeine. We will
fight over who gets to choose the next cd
while you tell me that I listen to too much
'chick music'. We will study the maps of our
bodies under dim light at a Days Inn, travel
the roads slowly and memorize every destination
so we never forget our way home.

Like salvation

And here is the jar of stars I've
collected - your name etched
into each glowing corner. And here
is the pulse of my wrist against the
soft flesh of your legs, a reminder
of devotion, the Morse code of an
unspoken truth. And here are the
arms I travel like memory, like the
record playing over and over into
the deep corners of evening. And
here is the weight of what I carry
each day, in all of the inches of
skin, in the name of this perfect
thing we cannot name, but know to
be our reason to open tired eyes,
to hold like a newborn - like salvation.

I've come around this time to set fire to your bones

to lay waste to any inhibition, to use your legs
as a ladder—a slow climb to deep breaths. Skin
is a barrier torn down, a breached railroad crossing—
gates down, gates crashed, lights blinking furiously.
Our staccato rhythm, our early spring headboard soundtrack—
a rush of frenzied guitar strings blasting from internal
amps. We watch the rise and fall in collapse, see the
vapor radiate off flesh. The walls are an engulfed wasteland
holding us in fortress. We watch the curtains drop ash to
the floor, and strike another match.

We are made of so much hunger

and it leaves us balled up against
the painted paneling of a cold room,
the wind pummeling trees and gutters
while we rock and stare, while we
hold ourselves in the quiet of a
November afternoon. We are made of
unquenchable desire, unable to find
bodies to consume, left to drag dry
fingers over smudged screens in hope
of consolation. We bruise ourselves
inside and out, then cover blemishes
with careful precision—the damaged
fruit that we are. We are both sweet
and bitter on the inside, desperate
and crippled with any brush, with the
slightest show of affection. Our plates
are hardened with the remnants of all
we can no longer have, all we still
desperately need.

For a second, I actually felt sunshine in the moss of me

It penetrated through the deep shag and gave
the roots an awakening. It stirred me to rise,
to stare through its insistent glow, to find
the bravery to let the worn pads of my feet
touch the chilled wood floor. I felt the glow
spread across my bare skin, as you stretched
your blanket warmed limbs around me, spoke no
words, and coaxed me to tangle with your small
frame, to disappear in your brilliance and
consume the whole of you.

A deep blue sky

keeps you held in protection
as you race over remote, two
laned highways—your golden
strands waving through the
sunroof, sending you past the
ever changing terrain. We want
caution erased from our dialect,
want fingers and lips to send us
to places we've feared more than
falling. You yank the rear view
mirror off of the windshield, and
toss it on the floor behind you
to mingle with empty water bottles
and scattered notebooks that have
written our next chapter. The space
in the months before become a blur,
become an archive labeled *before us*.

I really like you

In here is the reveal:
disbelief suspended in
quiet moments away from
the adoration of online
droves. Here, I have a
moment. Here, I confess
that your voice waltzes
in my brain, that your
preciousness can transform
this hardened face into
softened clay. You could
be my sweet revelation,
but I'm so in my head,
and every song in my brain
is your voice on repeat,
is the definition of sweet.

You are the smell before rain

the expectation
of dampness, of cleansing
and renewal.
You are the rush
of water bursting through
a downspout,
the rise of steam from
hot asphalt, a release
and a shudder.
You are all languid limbs
and open mouthed—
a whirlpool swallowing me
whole.

Squall

You were the afternoon storm
that blew in unannounced, tore
shingles off of roof tops, and
left me soaked and desperate
for your fingers to brush my
wet face. You are the thirst at
2 am that cannot be quenched,
the outline of a girl that I want
drawn into my daydreams. You
are the sweet scent in my lungs,
the hunger that never leaves.

I want to be your favorite destination

the cabin behind the thick trees,
halfway up a mountain that you
drive through mist and clouds for.
I want to be the bed that gets to
hold your curves at night, that
gets to feel you rise in the morning.
I want to be your favorite coffee
mug, the stream of light through the
opening in the curtains that warms
you on a crisp Spring morning. I want
to be your blanket, wrapped in your
radiance.

Please take me away from here

and take me to a Starbucks for a
lemonade iced tea, where we'll
give fake names, where we'll share
a warmed up cookie on the outside
patio and watch the wind blow carts
and old flyers into the air. Please
take me to a motel in a quiet farm
town off of a two laned highway
where we can curl up on a king sized
bed with candy wrappers and half
empty chip bags outlining our bodies,
where we can stretch single fingers
towards the middle, touch, and see
a lifetime like a giant projector on
the ceiling. Please take me away to
a deep sleep, our bodies fitted like
pale sheets, where dreams aren't a
stop and start, where the beginning
and the end are same, where we live
in pictures we never delete, in
moments left inside of us like words
deeply embedded in tree bark and stone.

Run away with me

In the daydream, your lips tasted
like fresh strawberries, and we rode
bicycles down city streets. Your long,
dark hair soaked in the spring's warm
sun. At midnight, we found each other
again, under teardrop shaped streetlights.
We packed our bags with things like body
butter and Skittles, saved just enough
room for toothbrushes and our favorite
shirts. This time, your kisses tasted
like sea salt and ocean swells. We drive,
blasting our favorite songs as a soundtrack
to a new life. You promise a world turned
to gold. *We never sleep. We never try.*

II.   The shadowboxers burned into wallpaper as silhouettes, as ghosts

Twenty three

At 23, you flew to Kansas City, read
poems at Charlie Parker's grave. At
23, I was saddled to someone with an
eye for my best friend. At 23, you've
published a chapbook. At 23, I was
working three jobs, saving nothing.
At 23, you have created an arts scene
in your town from nothing, rose above
the trappings of addiction and malaise.
At 23, I watched friends peel away from
me like dead skin. At 23, you possess
a fire of creativity. At 23, I had given
up on writing. At 23, you are already a
greater presence than I'll ever be.

You are tectonic plates awakened
(for Ryan)

It is the alien underneath your skin
that gives you unrest at night,
turns holding a fork, a pen, a hand
into a battle with an invisible force.
It is the second, third, fourth and fifth
opinions that mirror each other.
It is the crossing of fingers that the
next bottle will hold the pills that
will quell the seismic activity in your arm.
It is the dueling forces of sadness and
optimism—the arms of your wife, your son
that keep the ground from opening,
from swallowing you.

Ain't no sunshine
(for Brooke)

You gather the pieces of her,
spread them on the table in
front of you like cards, like
keepsakes kept in a music box:
tiny baby shoes,
little t-shirts that she
has long forgotten.
Her baby scent still lingers
in the smallest spot of her head,
in the memories you have planted,
where you can open it like a book
and inhale while your eyes are flush
with tears. Time is a plane ride,
a descent into cities of sunshine,
of smog, of dreams alive and dying.
Distance is a phone call, the grasp
over miles that cannot loose itself,
that will always be the softest pillow,
the long embrace over the skinned knees
and shattered hearts life will deal her.
She will once again run across the
sand. You will see her face this time.

Breathe, don't speak
(for Shaindel)

and watch the rise and fall of
your son's chest as he sleeps—
the best parts of your ex form
his laugh, his half smile. Don't
speak, and loose the blows from your
insides, the pieces of deception
and closed fist explanations.
Breathe, and set ablaze the verse
that keeps bald tires spinning in
place, that is a broken GPS signal
sending you repeatedly back to the
myopic eyes of broken boys who never
became men. Breathe, and bloom in
the bright August sun, the finches
cooling themselves with your spigot.
Breathe your words across screens
and never apologize for your light.

Even after I die
(for Attrell)

There were pieces removed:
a leg, lost to diabetes,
movement, reduced by the
earthquake in your brain,
now a sealed vault. Did
your detractors cripple
the music in your head?
Was being immobile like
a prison—a place where
the notes played sharply,
unorganized and scattered?
Did you know that your
cousin would claim what
you built for his own
selfish needs—a pathetic
attempt to pull your star
into his own barren orbit?
Your body showed mercy at
the end, let you sleep
painless and unknowing.
Now, people finally speak
of your genius—your keen
musical knowledge. There is
a small legacy you leave
with those who were drawn
into the sweeping melodies,
the words of deep loss and
repentance, of penitence.

Today is a good day

Today, you wore purple superhero
lipstick. Today, you were happy
with how your bangs fell over your
face. Today, your picture had forty
likes on Facebook. Today, you didn't
worry about your skin, and how it
sometimes bursts with the redness of
anxiety. Today, you didn't think about
how your rapist was stalking you a few
months ago. Today, the thoughts about
stepping in front of a moving car, the
relief in your head of a last breath
ceased. Today, you can hate yourself a
little less. Today, your brightness
stretched over the prairies—into the
soft caress of morning sun.

Something other than the darkness

You discard each piece of clothing
like candy wrappers onto the cold,
smooth tiles, watch them gather as
threaded eyes still peering at your
form, as a reminder to become kindling.
You cannot wash senses from your memory,
cannot kill the lingering scent of gin
from behind your ears, where his breathing
was its heaviest. You gather yourself at
the bottom of a shower, run bristles and
mesh fibers over your cells. You still
smell his scent, still feel his sweat over
your reddening skin. There are acres of
trees surrounding your shelter. He cannot
navigate through them, cannot slink miles
up the coast to steal another piece of you.
You bury him deep inside a vault that holds
every broken man's insecurities, learn to
fall in love with a bathtub again. The hand
that reaches for your face now holds your
exhaling, cradles a shared heartbeat, traces
the shape of infinity in your outline.

Lindsay moves to New Mexico

After the escape from your abusive
ex-boyfriend. After erasing your
name and choosing a new one. After
your body is felled by itself, by
something the size of a fist that
sent you on multiple trips to the
emergency room. After the catheter.
After being filmed reading one of
your poems, nude, with the catheter.
After working on your next sad
machine of a chapbook. After your
body fails you again, without any
warning. After the pain subsides.
After you eat all of the Hobnobs.
After you visit Alcatraz. After
you explode thinking about the
people you love. After the world
ends. After the makeout session is
done.

Warning Call
(for Mia)

It is the gasp and twist,
the turned body pushing a sore
hip into springs. The pain, a
prelude to system failure,
to the slow wind down uneven
roads dusted with crushed plastic
bottles and discarded pennies.
It will attach deep inside flesh,
feed off of unseen pieces. It will
manifest in the gait, in the way
a body curls into the soft middle
of a recliner. Injections can only
ward off the inevitable for so long.
Ache will disappear—like the dark
brown of eyes, like hair, like the
whistling sound of sleep breathing
on a rainy Wednesday, when the word
Remembering appears next to a name,
now exhaling in finality.

Saturday night in Montclair

Charlie monopolizes the ashtray
and sits at the end of the sofa
with the window open. The wall
above him is lined with framed
vinyl lp's, and he's rubbing
Sadie's belly, and then leans
in, resting his ear to her chest.
"She sounds congested. I think
we're giving her lung cancer,"
he says, as he carries the weight
of the pug's burdens. Kathleen
decides to listen herself, but
doesn't hear anything. Charlie may
be more obsessed with morbid
thoughts than I am, as he lights
up another Marlboro Gold, which
used to be called Marlboro Lights
before the government decided that
anything called "Light" was nothing
more than deceiving the public. K
tells us that Sadie is deaf now,
that it's a matter of time before
she's blind, as well, but it doesn't
seem to phase her. She can still
smell the meatballs and pasta we're
eating in the living room. She still
knows her mom's scent, and where to
find the recycles to knock over again.
Charlie says that it was probably him
who made Sadie deaf from constantly
yelling at her, the ashtray slowly
filling with the remnants of his own
anxieties—each cigarette butt, another
albatross to count.

The rough earth
(for CM)

We both wade in shallow water,
looking for pennies, for keys
to a door that will lead us anywhere
other than where we are. I hold it
together with the words I release,
while your daughter's smile keeps
you from a path of melancholy that
you may never return from. Distance
keeps me bound to this chair, listening
to birds calling and bounding from tree
to tree looking for a partner to shutter
their eyes next to. I picture you wrapped
in the whitest sheets, impossibly twisted
in knots while dreaming, your restlessness
keeping you captive, while I stare at the
ceiling in the late hours of evening. We
stumble over each day like a raised block
of sidewalk, with no arms to keep us from
the cruel back hand of the rough earth.

Somewhere in Colorado
(for John)

My copy of our yearbook is probably
sitting in a landfill somewhere
here in New Jersey.
The thin, glossy pages curled,
water and sun damaged, faces fading
from them. You signed it at our
senior party, somewhere in the back,
though after all of this time, I
can't remember what you wrote. You
would have been among the few people
I would have talked to at our reunion
this year, had you made the trip from
Colorado back to Bergen County.
Now, you are a casualty
of a cursed graduating class—no longer
boys and girls, but lists of the pieces
of flesh that failed them. You are the
condolences that grow online, nostalgia
in grade school pictures. Now, you are
the embers of our childhood, the long
final release.

The writer questions his existence
(for Charlie)

It is the finished novel sitting
on a computer, the uncertainty
that whispers in your ear to move
to Kansas City, to Philadelphia,
to anywhere far enough away from
each let down you've cataloged in
a small notebook in your office.
It is your baritone in boomerang,
between the walls of a coffeeshop,
the meatballs you mold with care
in silence while the dog stares at
you, the sound of locks clicking.
It is the soles of shoes, worn and
tired of walking in the life of the
mundane, the cover of obscurity.

The balled fist inside your body
(for R)

You will abandon the self injections
for something that may cause the never
ending ache to subside. Your steps will
be more steady when you hike deep into
the woods, the yellow and red leaves
swallowing your silhouette. Your body
will stop attacking itself long enough
for you to steady your hands and capture
and post the scenery online. You think
about pushing rolling pins over dough—
stretching a bottom crust for a rhubarb
pie. You wonder if your arms will ache
a little less when the time comes to hold
your first grandchild. You think of co-pays
and codependence. You drift back to when
a bottle of Boone's and a clove cigarette
tasted sweet on your lips—how lying in bed
was movement and sweat, not paralysis and
fear. You listen to what your body tells
you—slow down or I will do that for you—
the itch and freeze climbing your legs,
know that the trails get steeper from here.

When the grief becomes more tangible in verse
(for Sierra)

And this is the grass your paws pounced
on in chase of squirrels.
And this is the sofa you spun and spun
on, dropping down into the shape of a
comma.
And these are the blankets you loved,
in a pile and missing the shape and
scent of you.
And this is the breeze carrying you off
to somewhere we can't locate on GPS.
And this is the lap you rested your tired
head in—empty and missing your warmth.
And these are the corners of an apartment—
emptied of affection, hiding grief in
drawers and empty food bowls.
And this is the pain,
the pain,
the pain held by your mom,
who tries to tape together her torn paper heart.

After the clearing

In my closets are all of the ghosts
that stretch their limbs around me
when the lights are out. Strewn on
my desk are half, and nearly finished
books whose words are contentment.
I have the ache in my shoulder that
has outlasted you—my depression still
speaks to me, has drowned out memories
of your covenant. I have the hum through
vents, the snap of my ankle when I walk.
I am not comfortless, and you are vapor
after the clearing.

When they broke your body
(for ERR)

You are all wilting daisies in
a vase devoid of water, long
stems weary from travel, from
the drag of pain from your
thighs to the bottom of your
calves. The weight of sickness,
the bearing down, the strain.
I hear the mourning—through the
haphazard pedals, through minor
notes struck. Inspiration is a
heavy ocean, a protection from
drowning. You wind through cities,
say that stable and normal are
the real fantasies, search for
natural beauty in the fringes of
every landscape.

Ambivalence breeds in suburbia

Annabelle sits in an office somewhere in
Bucks County wondering why her husband
is such an asshole. She fires small flares
online looking for someone to distract her
from texting him. She says he is her first,
her only. She says that she can't just toss
twenty one years in the trash. How many
of those years were you happy, Annabelle?
Are you resigning yourself to twenty one
more in the silence of your bedroom? Will
the voices on your tv be comforting enough
when the weight of his neglect bears down
like the sun in July? Is your own touch enough
to make you shudder with delight, make
your heart pound like a first date? Her words
fall silent. Annabelle pushes down the urges
to unburden herself, to think that a second
chance at love is possible. She will go home,
in the car she's still paying for, make his
dinner, blend in with the peeling wallpaper.

Seeking distraction

You are the empty bottles on
the floor on a Sunday night,
the disregard for what it will
bring in the morning. You are
the heaving after the guilt
after the dinner, the dessert,
the lack of attention from a
husband who would rather play
video games. You are the thin
slice of sharpened steel, the
acid reflux that has you bent
over in agony. You are untouched,
in a purgatory that leaves you
seeking distraction, needing
the brush and thrust of flesh.
You are the forgotten flower
between the pages of a long
ignored book—unquenched and
obscured.

Tired eyes
(for K.T.)

As if sharing a birth month is
tantamount to sharing the dull
ache of desolation. As if the
plaintive nature of your voice
could act as an embrace, as a
balm. As if the simplicity of
your words could induce a kind
of tsunami in my body, a crumble
of stagnant structure carefully
built to sustain this stunted
fervor. As if a connection of
brown and blue eyes could know
how deep sorrow could burrow.

Pruning
(for C.J.)

Loss is a pocket watch
that slowly ticks again
after winding. It is the
scab that will reside on
the side of your thumb—
a reminder that daughters
and grandchildren need
only seconds to disappear.
You watch the slow movement
of hands while bodies fall
away like a landslide, like
a late frost that snuffs a
March bloom. These late life
days have become longer—
a pocket filled with garden
stones. Your family tree,
a victim of the cruelest pruning.

III. Shattered mirrors and blackened Polaroids

The poet compiles a spreadsheet of loss

I am unpulled crabgrass,
an overgrown eye sore that
lingers in a state of flux.
This deep pressure is the
void left by those who exist
in name only, who will never
know what I held for them
beneath my tongue. Words
are faded ink, are pieces of
torn notes held prisoner in
old shoeboxes. Words are the
heart, a used up muscle, the
stupid, wide open arms that
gave and gave, now stay closed,
sore and empty.

The poet reflects on aging

The body is a chipped glass,
a stretched tendon, the bruising
of bone. It is the toss and turn,
the deep ache just above the waist,
the slow, limping walk to the bathroom.
The body is a crunch, a crack, a push
of ligaments to a rubber band's snap.
It is the discovery of new levels of
agony, the methodical trudge through
overgrown weeds. It is the rumble of
gases from the core, the eye of the
hurricane, the kiss before the stab.

Poet as an abandoned building

In here, there was a steady pulse,
a rhythmic lifeline. Now, the
hinges squeak, the pulse is a slowed
thump, a strain. There are papers
strewn about inside the eyes, words
in scattershot, forming a language
only translated by their creator.
No one visits anymore. Insects have
abandoned the long, cavernous halls.
There is plant life above in two tone,
in winding, blondish waves of reckless
brush. Soon, the roof will cave in.
Soon, it will immolate.

The poet reflects on commitment

We own the aches we wake with.
We eat banana pancakes in mid
morning, stretch our bodies
into desk chairs and listen to
the passing cars, as books pile
and a mountain of mulch remains
unmoved in front of the curb.
This week moves with greater
intent than we want it to, and
the inevitable return to routine
looms. We gather our bones, the
presents to each other, avoid
counting the days that remain.
We become wistfulness, a number
that grows. We watch scenery
shift, our roots thick and buried
deep in the wet earth.

The poet reflects on convenience

In between conventions,
selfies with actors I do
not know, hair experiments,
cat pictures and cosplays,
you send a short, random
message-
Hi. I miss you.
You, the small lurker,
the distant constant.
You, the emotional waterfall,
the universal empath.
What am I thinking right now?

The poet reflects on empty verses

They are Insta-poets, they are fast
food poets, poets of platitudes, poets
who are as deep as a wading pool, a
puddle that tadpoles would avoid. They
are the opposite of work, of literary
students, of the passion that embodies
an artist. They are the sneeze that does
not get a gesundheit, the tissue to wipe
the nose. They are living, breathing
Pinterest pages, notebook paper with one
question mark in the middle.

The poet reflects on lost friendship

You once told me that
I was the only one you
could confide in—that
the times you tried to
kill yourself at college,
the abuse you suffered
at the hands of your long
time boyfriend, the fear
of ending up like your
alcoholic mother, were
things that have never
passed through your lips
to anyone else. You held
our friendship like a
wounded dog, like a
newborn. Now, you are the
paper boat sinking in dirty
river water, waiting to
submerge, to no longer be.

The poet reflects on mortality

I have always imagined my death
to be brutal—multiple gun shots
during a robbery—a massive heart
attack while driving—a spectacular
car wreck where I'm mangled beyond
recognition. In truth, a quiet passing
on the sofa, feet raised, deep within
a dream, would be ideal, but no one
gets to choose. No one hates me
enough to kill me. The distance I keep
from people is my barrier against a
murder of passion. The thought of
no longer breathing a deep breath in
the quiet of evening is strange enough
to contemplate, but almost a comfort
to the constant feeling of being the
discarded wrapper, decaying against
a curb, the afterthought left abandoned.

The poet reflects on ownership

Each of these cells covering me
are owned—by the eight hours a
day given to thankless labor,
by the corporations that want me
to give them everything earned to
simply exist. I watch numbers grow
zeros at the ends of bills, watch
the air I breathe tax me for use
in excess. I hear grumblings from
the homes of people who do not even
know my name, nor care to. Forced
opinions at work are called jokes,
are tucked away in cabinet drawers
as nonchalance grows. I will duck
under the street light cameras, let
my license expire, carry rolls of
coin. I will become vagabond, become
nomadic. My existence will become a
bonfire, a trail of decomposed words.

The poet reflects on hearing her voice for the first time

She is on the verge of breakdown,
on the ledge where a waterfall of
sobs will rain down. This is not
contrived emotion. This is the
sound of someone whose words are
too heavy to carry, who cannot bear
to keep them held inside of her.
I picture us in the longest embrace—
with her words, my words, spilled
like glitter all over the floor,
our shoulders wet with the release
of emotion. I picture my hands
cupping her face, her eyebrows in
a downward arch, knowing that she
will never be done bleeding this
wound, that sometimes, a catalog
of casualties is all one has left
to hold.

IV.   *The shards that remain, scattered over dirt and asphalt.*

In her leaving

And the truth was a spinning saw blade,
the push in front of a speeding train.
It ended with a whisper, a barricade.
There was no time for a detailed letter,
a tearful, contrived goodbye. There was
only the throbbing in the head, the slow
beat of a heart stretched beyond its means.
It was the last gasp, the figure of a girl
leaving behind detachment, leaving behind
the despondent carcass of a man.

A purpose

You are the shrunken ice cubes
melting in the drain screen—
the invisible husk that walks
hunched between trees and over
trash and goose shit littered
suburban side streets. In the
busy air of afternoon, only the
birds will notice your descent
into the forest. Steel does not
make noise, and the ground will
consume what it is fed, will take
even the most useless parasites,
and give them a purpose.

In the wake of running

Wedged between the carefully laid
words is an aberration—a blind
reveal that has changed the landscape.
I am held breath, shattered bottles
in front of a chipped curb. You are
the scattered crowd, the fallout
shelter. The doors have been bolted
and sealed. In my hands, the last
gasp, the means to an end.

In the garden of damaged people

The shovel is on the verge
of snapping. The fiberglass
handle cannot take the constant
use. You have buried so much in
this yard—dead birds, poems,
hope for a future. You find a
spot on the side of the house,
crack the earth, push the metal
deep into the ground with the
heel of your foot. You dig thick
fingers into the skin of your
chest, pull the beating muscle
out. You stare at how purple it
looks in the sunlight, toss it
carelessly into the hole in the
ground. It is already home to
sow bugs and worms, already a
grave. You want to grow something
harder, something that can resist
ache, something that will not split
down the middle. You water it with
whispers of promise, curl up on the
disturbed ground, ask for absolution
from the emptiness. The ground is
tainted, may never grow another
heart.

Incineration

There are times I sit in line
with the brightest afternoon
sunlight, in hopes that I will
burst into flames, that the
pasty skin of my arms will
blister and burn, my freckles
will turn to spark. I wish this
only to be a spectacle for one
moment, to bask in some sort
of spontaneous supernova, to
become something other than
the wilting flower in the side
of my garden where nothing
grows, or ever will.

I am making my loneliness small
(after Chen Chen)

enough to fit folded in my front
left pocket, behind the empty
wallet that holds everything
needed to identify me when the
last pieces of bone are found.
I am making the loneliness a
fresh pot of coffee, leaving the
vanilla creamer on the kitchen
counter, though I know he won't
put it back in the fridge. I am
writing him a poem he will judge
like the prick that he is. I am
holding my phone up above me for
another horrid selfie, and he is
snickering behind me in the back
right corner. I am taking my
loneliness on a road trip, on a
hike into deep wilderness. We will
sit in the black of evening, count
the number of barking dogs and
fade from existence, like breath.

Pop life

They will want to dig up everything
imaginable when you die. There will
be questions about your son's death,
why both of your marriages failed,
why you have thousands of songs in
a vault. Some will cry out of genuine
grief for how your artistry moved
them, how it was the soundtrack of
a part of their lives that they are
suddenly nostalgic about now that
you're dead. Some will want to know
how you managed to get addicted to
painkillers, why you couldn't just
stop taking something that quelled
the pain for so long that you had
no idea how to live without it. They
will play your most popular album,
as it's the only one they own, fuck
up the lyrics to every song, profess
how they were such huge fans. No one
will speak of your generous heart, of
the people you helped out of poverty,
the fact that you taught yourself how
to play over twenty instruments. In
the year since your passing, sales of
nearly all of your albums leapt into
the stratosphere, yet no one was there
to breathe life back into you while you
slowly slipped away on the floor.

All the possible scenarios

What if I were to drag the sharpest
blade in the kitchen drawer over the
blue pulsing rivers of my wrist? What
if the act of breathing could be held
in a sort of suspension, a stifled tea
kettle ready to burst? What if the
sound of crying could be muffled by
the weight of pills? What if bones could
catch fire inside flesh and skin? What
if a beginner's swan dive were his last?
What if a creek became a blanket, the
deep sleep that becomes an eternal dream?

Us, as verse

Does the poem disintegrate slowly,
as we do, in the ways our breathing
changes, as our hearts beat in a new
rhythm? Does the poem get rewritten
so many times that it loses strength,
that it is as profound as greeting
card verse, that floors begin to
buckle from growing weight? Does the
poem keep us in freeze frame, or does
it write us out of existence? Does it
send us to the same moment repeatedly,
and do we find solace in familiarity?
Is the poem the beginning or the end?

You are a foot bridge

over an endless freshwater lake,
a thick fog clouding my sight line.
Your legs are the lamp posts, the
lights either flickering or blown
entirely. Your arms are bullets of
thick rain, are the thunder, and
your mouth is the lightning, pieces
of electricity materialized in the
graying sky. His arms are the thief.
Your frame—the embrace I will never feel.

Carrion

And what becomes of someone who
spends days sacrificing pieces of
their body until there is nothing
left at the altar but blood? Does
the cathedral grow a new skin?
Will holy water run red? We will
carve a plaque, build a monument
to commemorate your gifts of
sanity and satiation. We will hold
a vigil for your lost sleep, for the
fingers flayed trying to hold on
to arms that swung like flailing
branches in a hurricane. What does
a body do when it has become a
roadside carcass, unwanted carrion?

I've started thinking of people as wounds that don't heal

as scabs that harden, then break open at the worst
possible moments, and bleed down pale skin like a
pierced apple, slowly. I've started thinking about
the desperation some people gather like bloomed
flowers, and plant deep inside their chests—how
expectation is the set up pitch, the fast ball that
blurs the hopefulness held in the most tender of
places. I've started thinking that I am a broken
yardstick, protruding out of rain soaked earth in
a barren backyard—that all measurements of desire
are inaccurate, are the runoff racing down smoothed
concrete, destined for a sewer grate, for the ocean,
a storm's casualty.

Can you smell the silence on my breath?

the words have dissipated into
 the sharp angles of
      walls and door frames
into the thin layer
 of dust under a marred
      telephone table that creaks
when I rest the weight of my
 body, the gravity of failure into
      the distressed legs of wood.

All of the rain that has fallen cannot clean
this covering of concession, of collapse.

This smell is the burnt
 crust of resignation that
      lingers like a dead skunk on
yellow double lines on a country road.

Opened windows will never clear the stench
of death from memory.

We are always trespassers

rapping at screen doors
at four in the morning,
throwing pebbles at a
window just to see a
silhouette of our
affection, to find
soil rich enough to
fill the crater sized
gaps in our chests. We
listen for the creaking
of old wood and hinges in
need of oil, look for the
breath gathering in a cloud
on a brisk fall evening, when
an infiltration becomes the last
hope of organs no longer able to
sustain the weight of punishment,
of this punching bag existence.

Under this windless sky

I call for the stillness of bodies
in the vicinity of my hands,
the cold brush of leaving,
a phone number erased from
a whiteboard, from memory.
Everything I have touched has
found an exit: death, disposal,
an abandoned haunting.
I choose to kick all traces of
love into the holes of a sewer grate,
to forget how to gather a frame
between the sharp pain coursing in
this failing vessel. Thirst is the
only familiar, and it will always
hide what can quench me, always leave
me abandoned in a town that is
near death.

Some days I want to sit in my sadness like a parked car
(after Emilia Phillips)

Some days, I want to sit in my sadness
like a parked car, idling in front of
the nondescript ranch that, on most
days, will keep my body inside of it,
pushed into a corner like the crappy
prizes at the bottom of an old, cardboard
Cracker Jack box. Some days, I want the
sadness to consume me, to keep me from
the inevitable letdown after a temporary
high. The sadness knows every corner of
this crumbling structure. It knows when
to whisper its choruses, like the saddest
songs that I love—*I don't need you anyway,
I don't need you, go home*—or—*I think I used
to have a purpose, but then again, that might
have been a dream.* The sadness follows me
from room to room, like my dog looking for
food, for attention, watching to make sure
that my mouth does not make the slightest
upturn. I watch it swallow the rest of the
day from my window, listen for the sounds
of people closing car doors, racing from
the mundane to envelop themselves in bright
lights and distractions. I will stay shackled
with sadness, sharing sweet wine straight from
the bottle, watching blur become black.

Ripe bananas

are still useful for muffins
or bread, for begging dogs,
are easier to peel, the
darkening skin, spotted and
dying. Everything darkens
when it's ready to die—is a
faded picture of vibrancy.
The smell has overtaken
the dining room, is a death
knell. I peel layers of clothes
from tired bones, stare at
the stretching skin of my
wrist, research practical
uses for this bruised fruit.

This body catalogs each day it hasn't been touched
(after Trista Mateer)

in a small, dollar store date book
that is cracking at the spine.
There are circles around every day,
x's next to the numbers when you
fell asleep before me, check marks
for when I looked to strangers on
the internet for solace, for some
kind of dirty talk. I have run out
of days to write on.

V.   *When a body becomes invisible, becomes air.*

Alternate reality where

I am not simultaneously
distracted and repulsed
by the bloat occupying
the mirror, where the
bloat cannot manifest,
where a giant magnet can
erase shame and regret,
where people move in reverse,
and return over and over,
where I am able to say no,
and no, and no again and
again, where a body can be
an oak tree, a bloom of
green in April, where the
outside does not betray the
inside, where sleep is not
a shattered mosaic in a
run down, abandoned museum,
where a body is no longer
an undiscovered satellite,
drifting languidly.

The constellations are fading

They are descending into
a plodding death, swallowed
by the expanse of black
that will consume each of us.
Remembrance is a shattered
bottle, carelessly littered
over forgotten country roads.
We once danced like the most
brilliant of lights, seen only
in the most remote regions—
a treasured locket that held
heartbeats and promises,
but all stars explode.

The people you love become ghosts inside of you

that wander around the thick walls within
your beating heart, the low hum behind the
steady pulse of blood. You keep the best
of their existence like a 35mm movie behind
your eyes, and watch it on a loop in the
black of a January night, when absence eats
away at your stomach lining, when the skin
of your hands becomes tight and dry. Memory
becomes a trick—it leaves you yearning for
a tangible body, a voice that does not break
and drop out over phone lines. The people
you love become vapor, become steam escaping
a kettle—the page that erases itself.

The pain is evident in my existence

as my gait becomes folly,
as steps become a manifest
of torture, as the gravity
of inaction pushes on the
softening vertebra, as I
watch creeks become rivers
I wade further into, as
the swell of skin becomes
a threat, as I am held only
in evening's chill, in the
memory of everything and
everyone that has loosed
from my weakened grip.

Threesome

but not—
instead,
a demolition,
the wrecking
ball that
bashes the
joints and
beams. It was
never meant as
reality, as
perversion—
instead,
quiet adoration,
left as shame,
left as being
buried under the
rubble of a game.
A debasing—you
hide in your odium.

I can no longer hear home music

beneath the distant bangs unidentified
and the revved engines, speeding by and
kicking up tiny pebbles, tires crunching
against cracked asphalt. This house is
under water, under siege, under the spell
of March crickets emerging after a long
freeze. All of the wires have been pulled
from speakers, have been knotted and tossed
into trash cans that reek of spoiled things,
of fermented grass and old bags of dog shit.
What will I hear now that notes have been
replaced by high pitched ringing? Will the
earth open up in front of the maple tree in
the backyard and swallow me? I feel a burial
in the hollow of my bones, and I am ready.

Hard lesson

Your heels are dug into worn rugs,
into a continuous loop that sends
people through a revolving door.
You will lose them when they reach
the escalator—their bodies carried
into an abyss of white light. Their
names are held in storage, pulled
out with a sigh, a clinging to the
inflection of their voices, how a
written line can burrow into bone.
*Everyone you love will die before
you* becomes a mantra for a bio, for
a tombstone. You focus a watchful
eye on the calendar's flip, how a
countdown is a letdown, the slowest
shutdown. You grow loss like
wildflowers.

The skin is a language of pain

as it dries and hardens with
each loss, as it flakes and
pains under cold blasts. The
skin is a road map of a dying
city, is the rough terrain now
abandoned in the rebirth of
spring. The skin is goosebumped
topography, is the shiver and
recoil, is a wrinkled web of
regret—a whispered vernacular.

Specter

Names disappear like a clear
cut through my brain, like
disappearing ink, like the
hour lost every spring.
There is no space left in a
body excavated of ghosts for
an exercise in nostalgia.
The throb of vacancy is the
only familiar—a parasite to
carry into the unforgiving
and shortening days.

I've given up on sunlight

on the warmth that settles
inside the chest, on the
silhouette of shared euphoria.
I've given up on softness,
on breath caught in a bottle
on a foot printed beach. I've
given up on reciprocity, on
inherent kindness, on the idea
that the weakening bones within
me are worthy of affection. I've
given up on gathering afternoon's
brilliant shine, as I watch the
fall of evening slowly swallow
the whole of me.

Swallowed

Does a body exist if it is
only fluent in silence?
Will it trend on social
media? Will it be found in
a routine wellness check?
Will the organs be found
to have decayed long before
hands and eyes stopped moving?
Can the weight of cessation
be the impetus for a sort of
book burning, a return of
atoms to the universe's open,
insatiable mouth?

Write clear and true about what hurts

the fractured bones that healed in
a mass, the times you were left
crumpled and shattered, curled like
a sowbug, face down in blue carpet.
Write about the loneliness that digs
caverns in your chest, the sound a
shattered heart makes, over and over.
The unforgiving reflection, the inhale
and exhale. The emptiness of hands,
the chill and shiver of a desolate
landscape, left in disrepair.

I need more than words

I need the break of morning through
a curtain with a loosed string. I
need the sounds of all of the voices
that spur my fingers to create, that
lift my frayed resolve from sorrow.
I need the embrace, the elixir from
empty promises and platitudes. I need
to watch all of the streetlights on
my block simultaneously burn out,
have the night sky be lit only by
constellations. I need the rush—
the euphoria of something words could
never define, an unbridled bliss that
can return me to stardust, happily.

Kendall A. Bell's poetry has been most recently published in Kissing Dynamite and Dark Marrow. He was nominated for Sundress Publications' Best of the Net collection in 2007, 2009, 2011, 2012, 2013, 2015 and 2018. He has released 25 chapbooks and two full length collections. He is the founder and co-editor of the online journal Chantarelle's Notebook and publisher/editor of Maverick Duck Press. His chapbooks are available through Maverick Duck Press. He lives in Southern New Jersey.

www.ingramcontent.com/pod-product-compliance
Lightning Source LLC
LaVergne TN
LVHW091226080426
835509LV00009B/1187